Girls Science Club

Cool Biology Activities for Girls

by Kristi Lew

Consultant:
Laura L. Hoopes
Biology Professor
Pomona College
Claremont, California

CAPSTONE PRESS
a capstone imprint

Snap Books are published by Capstone Press,
1710 Roe Crest Drive, North Mankato, Minnesota 56003.
www.capstonepub.com

Copyright © 2012 by Capstone Press, a Capstone imprint.
All rights reserved.
No part of this publication may be reproduced in whole or in part, or stored in a retrieval system,
or transmitted in any form or by any means, electronic, mechanical, photocopying, recording,
or otherwise, without written permission of the publisher.
For information regarding permission, write to Capstone Press,
1710 Roe Crest Drive, North Mankato, Minnesota 56003.

 Books published by Capstone Press are manufactured with paper containing at least 10 percent post-consumer waste.

Library of Congress Cataloging-in-Publication Data
Lew, Kristi.
Cool biology activities for girls / by Kristi Lew.
p. cm.—(Snap books. Girls science club)
Summary: "Provides step-by-step instructions for activities demonstrating biology concepts and scientific explanations of the concepts presented"—Provided by publisher.
Includes bibliographical references and index.
ISBN 978-1-4296-7676-2 (library binding)
ISBN 978-1-4296-8019-6 (paperback)
1. Biology—Juvenile literature. 2. Biology—Study and teaching—Activity programs. 3. Girls—Education—Juvenile literature.
I. Title. II. Series.
QH309.2.L39 2012
570.78—dc23   2011020490

Editorial Credits
Editor: Jennifer Besel
Designer: Heidi Thompson
Photo Stylist: Sarah Schuette
Scheduler: Marcy Morin
Production Specialist: Kathy McColley

Photo Credits:
All images Capstone Studio: Karon Dubke except: Shutterstock: blue67design, cover (drawn design), Dmitry Melnikov, cover (bottom), vector-illustrator, cover (top)

Printed in the United States of America in North Mankato, Minnesota.
032017   010318R

Table of Contents

Dolphins, Daffodils, and You 4
Color Me Pretty 6
Blow Me Up 8
The Eyes Have It 10
Ah-choo! 12
Mini Garden 14
Remember Me? 16
Enzyme Action 18
Cell-abrate! 20
Beady DNA 22
Banana DNA 26

Glossary 30
Read More 31
Internet Sites 31
Index 32

Dolphins, Daffodils, and You

What do horses, humans, and houseplants have in common? All these things are alive. They all need food, water, and a safe place to live. And they all have unique ways to get what they need to stay alive.

Biology is the study of living things. But if you think biology is all about frog guts, think again. Biologists study living things in all kinds of ways. They study how dolphins communicate. They examine the air we breathe. And they determine how the delightful daffodils in your flower bed bloom. Check out the experiments in this book to see just how beautiful and fun biology can be.

To have the most fun with these projects, just follow a few simple guidelines:
1. Read the project all the way through before you start.
2. Gather all the materials you need.
3. If you don't get the results you expect the first time, try it again. The experiment might work a different way the next time.
4. Have fun!

Color Me Pretty

Roses are red. Violets are blue. Make some flowers any color you want to!

Supplies

- 4 tall glasses
- lukewarm water
- red, green, yellow, and blue food coloring
- 4 spoons
- scissors
- 4 white flowers
- ruler
- vase

TIP: Any white flower will work, but carnations work best for this project.

1. Fill each glass about half-full with water.

2. Add 30 drops of red food coloring to one of the glasses. Use a spoon to mix the water and the food coloring together.

3. Add 30 drops of green food coloring to another glass. Stir with a different spoon.

4. Add 15 drops each of yellow and red food coloring to a third glass. Stir.

5. In the last glass, add 15 drops each of blue and red food coloring. Stir.

6. Cut each flower stem at an angle 2 inches (5 centimeters) from the bottom. Place one flower into each glass.

7. In a few hours, you should start to see color in the flowers' petals. Leave the flowers in the colored water overnight. The next day, take the flowers out of the colored water. Place them into a vase with fresh, clear water. Now you have a colorful bouquet to decorate your room.

Insider Info

Plants need food and water to survive. To get those nutrients, a plant **absorbs** what it needs from soil or water. Then the water moves up the flower's stem into its leaves and petals. The plant's leaves have tiny openings called stomata. Water **evaporates** from these tiny holes. In this project, the food coloring traveled up the stems with the water into the flowers' petals. The water evaporated, but the food coloring didn't.

absorb—to soak up
evaporate—to change from a liquid into a vapor or a gas

Blow Me Up

Who knew that blowing up balloons could be a science experiment? The next time you're having a party, test your lung power while you decorate.

Supplies
- permanent marker
- 2 balloons
- stopwatch

1. Using a marker, label one balloon with the number one. Label the other balloon number two.

2. Give both balloons a good stretch in all directions to make them easier to blow up.

3. With one breath, blow up balloon number one as much as you can. Tie off the end of the balloon.

4 Now run in place for three minutes.

5 As soon as time is up, take a deep a breath, and blow up balloon number two as much as possible. Tie off the end. Can you tell a difference between the two balloons?

Insider Info

This experiment measured your lung **capacity**. Your lung size affected how much air you blew into the first balloon. The second balloon you blew into was probably smaller than the first. Here's why. Your body's **cells** need oxygen to function properly. When you exercise your muscles need more oxygen than normal. To get more oxygen into your blood, you breathe heavier. All that huffing and puffing makes it hard to get a deep breath to blow up balloons.

capacity—the total amount something can hold
cell—the smallest unit of a living thing

The Eyes Have It

Do you flinch when something comes at you in a 3D movie? If so, you've seen how your brain and eyes work together. For 3D movies and this activity, two eyes are definitely better than one.

Supplies

- 3 washable markers—black, red, and blue
- poster board, 22 inches (56 cm) by 28 inches (71 cm)
- newspaper
- yardstick
- masking tape

1. With the black marker, draw a target on the poster board. The target should be made of three circles. The second and third circles should fit inside the larger outside circle.

2. Spread a layer of newspaper on the floor. Place the target on the newspaper. Make sure the newspaper shows around all sides of the poster board.

3. Measure 1 yard (.9 meter) from the edge of the poster board. Place a piece of masking tape at the 1-yard mark. Stand on the piece of tape. Have your friend stand next to the target, holding one arm out with the red marker tip down.

4 Close one of your eyes. Direct your friend to move forward, backward, or side to side until you think the marker is right above the center circle. Then tell your friend to drop the marker.

5 Repeat the marker drop four more times with the red marker. Keep one eye closed.

6 Now have your friend get the blue marker. Repeat steps 5–7, but keep both eyes open.

7 Count up how many marks of each color hit the center circle. Could you hit the center better using one eye or two?

Insider Info

Having two eyes gives humans and other animals depth perception. Depth perception allows you to tell which objects are closer to you and which are farther away. It is also what allows you to see objects in three dimensions (3D). Because your eyes are about 2 inches (5 cm) apart, they each get a slightly different view of things. Your brain uses these differences to determine about how far away something is. With only one eye, your brain doesn't get as much information. That makes it harder to hit the target's center.

Ah-choo!

That tickle in your nose isn't just an itch. It's a sign that you've breathed in something suspicious. Use these particle catchers to see what's in the air around you.

Supplies

- 6 3-inch by 5-inch (8-cm by 13-cm) index cards
- scissors
- ruler
- hole puncher
- 6 12-inch (30-cm) pieces of string
- wax paper
- 6 2-inch by 4-inch (5-cm by 10-cm) self-adhesive address labels
- magnifying glass

1 Fold one index card in half. Cut out a rectangle from the center, leaving a ¾-inch (2-cm) border on all sides. Unfold the index card. Now there's a "window" in the middle of the card. This piece is the frame.

2 Punch a hole in the middle of one of the frame's short sides. Measure and cut a piece of string. Thread the string through the hole, and tie the ends together.

3 Repeat steps 1 and 2 with the other five index cards.

4. Spread a piece of wax paper on a table. Place all of the frames on the wax paper. Peel one address label from its sheet. Center the label over the window in one of the frames. Press the label onto the frame. The center of the label will stick to the wax paper. Repeat with the remaining frames and labels.

5. Peel the frames away from the wax paper. Hang each collector in a different part of your house or yard.

6. Allow the collectors to hang in place for a week. Then take them down, and use your magnifying glass to find out what they've caught.

Insider Info

The things caught in your sticky catchers are called airborne particles. These particles can be tiny bits of things such as dust, pet dander, or pollen. Or they may be small droplets of liquid such as water or cooking oil. These particles float around in the air you breathe.

Your nose and throat are lined with **mucous membranes**. These sticky membranes catch the particles so they don't get into your lungs. Your nose hairs catch airborne particles too. You eventually swallow the stuff the membranes and hairs catch. The particles end up in your digestive system.

mucous membranes—a soft tissue in the body that creates a slimy fluid that coats the inside of a person's breathing passages

Mini Garden

Add a splash of color to your room with flowers and plants. With this project, you'll have a mini garden to bring the outdoors inside.

Supplies

- 1-gallon fishbowl with a large opening
- dish soap
- water
- dish towel
- small rocks
- ruler
- sphagnum moss
- potting soil
- 4 small houseplants
- small decoration such as a butterfly, animal, or house (optional)
- small watering can or glass

 **TIPS:** You should be able to find the sphagnum moss near the potting soil in most large stores. For the plants, herbs, spider plants, miniature begonias, African violets, and ferns work well.

1. Wash your fishbowl with hot, soapy water and allow it to dry completely.

2. Add a layer of small rocks about 1 inch (2.5 cm) thick to the bottom of the bowl. Then put about an inch (2.5 cm) of moss on top of the rocks.

3. Layer potting soil on top of the moss. Use enough soil to fill the bowl about half full. Dig four holes about 3 inches (8 cm) deep in the dirt with your fingers. Space the holes a few inches apart so the plants will have as much room as possible.

4 Remove the plants from their containers, and brush away most of the dirt from their roots. Place the plants into the holes. Put the tallest plants in back and the shorter ones in front.

5 Cover the roots with soil, and pat down the soil firmly. If you have a small decoration, place it in front of the plants.

6 Water the plants just enough to make the soil damp. Don't over water. The soil should not be soggy.

7 Keep your terrarium in an area where the plants get sunlight every day. Water the plants when the soil gets dry. If there is water between the rocks at the bottom, you don't need to water yet.

Insider Info

This tiny landscape is called a terrarium. A terrarium is a mini ecosystem, a collection of nonliving and living things that work together. The sphagnum moss helps keep moisture in the terrarium but allows the soil to drain. This drainage prevents the plants' roots from rotting in soggy soil. The soil provides the plants with the water and nutrients they need. Green plants need light to live too. They use energy from the sun, water from the soil, and gases from the air to make food. Outdoor plants also rely on the soil, water, and light in their surroundings to live. Indoors or out, plants will only grow big and strong when they get what they need from their environment.

Remember Me?

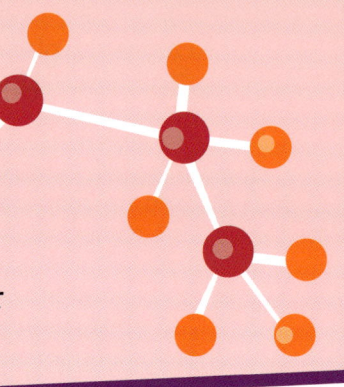

Want to mess with your friends' memories? Set up this experiment at your next party. See how many people remember things that aren't really there.

Supplies

- black marker
- poster board, 22 inches (56 cm) by 28 inches (71 cm)
- clear tape
- plain white paper
- pencils

1. Write the following words on the poster board in two columns.

   Column 1: star, planet, galaxy, sun, moon, night, sleep, cold, dark, gloves, hat, scarf, coat, rain

   Column 2: desk, bed, kitten, sleep, tent, rock, apple, light, night, music, forest, bell, mouse, lamp

2. Tape two or three sheets of paper together vertically. Tape the top piece of paper to the poster board, completely covering column one. Repeat for column two.

3. When you're ready to start the game, uncover column one. Give guests one minute to look at the word list.

4. When time is up, cover column one. Wait five minutes. Give each guest a pencil and paper. Then uncover column two.

5. Give guests one minute to write down any words that they think are on both lists.

6. When time is up, go through column two one word at a time. Did some people say "bed" and "light" were on list one? Uncover both lists. Only "sleep" and "night" appear on both lists.

Insider Info

When you first learn or do something, the information is stored in your short-term memory. Short-term memory can only hold about seven items at once. That's not much information. Most people naturally use a strategy called chunking to help them remember more. Chunking means to group information in familiar ways. For example, you might put the words star, planet, sun, and moon together. Someone else might chunk moon with night, sleep, cold, and dark.

But here's where memories get crazy. Sometimes when it's chunking information, the brain makes up its own memories. The word list included the words night and sleep. Many people will falsely remember the word bed as well. Scientists aren't exactly sure why this happens. But they believe it may have something to do with how our brains organize information.

Enzyme Action

Putting fruits in gelatin makes a tasty dessert. But add the wrong fruit, and you could be left drinking your Jell-O.

Supplies

- permanent marker
- masking tape
- 2 small bowls
- knife
- cutting board
- fresh pineapple
- measuring cups
- canned pineapple chunks in natural juices
- 2 3-ounce packages of gelatin, any flavor
- small saucepan
- spoon
- water

1. Use the marker to write the word "canned" on a piece of masking tape. Place the masking tape on the side of one bowl. Prepare another label that says "fresh." Put this label on another bowl.

2. Ask an adult to help chop the fresh pineapple into bite-sized chunks. Measure and pour ¾ cup (175 mL) fresh pineapple into the bowl labeled "fresh."

3. Drain the liquid from the canned pineapple. Measure and pour ¾ cup (175 mL) canned pineapple chunks in the bowl labeled "canned."

4 Have an adult help prepare one package of gelatin according to the package directions. Pour the hot, liquid gelatin into the bowl with the fresh pineapple. Prepare the second package of gelatin. Pour it into the bowl with the canned pineapple.

5 Place the containers in the refrigerator, and wait at least four hours. Did the gelatin set firmly in both bowls?

Insider Info

Gelatin is made up of long chains of **protein**. When these protein chains tangle, the gelatin sets. You get the wiggling, jiggling treat you expect. But fruits can mess with those protein chains. Fruits contain **enzymes** that break long protein chains into shorter ones. All fruits have some of these enzymes, but pineapples have more than most. When you put fresh pineapple into gelatin, the enzymes break down the gelatin's protein chains. The chains can't tangle, so the gelatin doesn't set.

The gelatin with the canned pineapple set because there weren't enzymes breaking apart the protein chains. Canned pineapple is heated in the canning process. Heat destroys enzymes. So there was nothing stopping the gelatin proteins from tangling up.

Why is this important? Your body has these enzymes too. Proteins enter your body through foods such as meat, cheese, eggs, and fish. Your digestive system uses enzymes to break down those proteins. Without this protein-breaking process, you couldn't get energy from food.

protein—a chemical found in cells that carries out various functions necessary for life
enzyme—a protein that helps break down food

Cell-abrate!

Eggs aren't just for breakfast and Easter decorations. Check out this egg stripping, shriveling, and plumping experiment. But plan ahead. This activity takes a few days to complete.

Supplies
- 2 raw eggs
- 3 medium plastic bowls with lids
- white vinegar
- slotted spoon
- corn syrup
- water

1. Carefully place the eggs into a bowl. Pour vinegar over the eggs until they are completely covered. Put the lid on the bowl. Leave the eggs in the vinegar for two days. The vinegar will **dissolve** the egg shells.

2. After the egg shells have dissolved, carefully remove the eggs from the vinegar with a slotted spoon. Place the eggs into two separate bowls.

3 In one bowl, cover the egg with corn syrup.

4 In the other bowl, cover the egg with water. Place lids on both bowls and leave overnight.

5 The next day, examine the eggs. Did one of them shrivel up while the other one got bigger?

Insider Info

All living things are made up of cells. Your body has trillions of cells. A chicken egg is a cell too. But it's much bigger and easier to see. A thin, flexible layer of tissue called a membrane surrounds all cells. When the shell is removed, the chicken egg is left with just a cell membrane. Cell membranes allow some chemicals to pass through while keeping others out. Water is one chemical that can go through a cell membrane.

The movement of water into or out of a cell through its membrane is called osmosis. Cells naturally contain water. In osmosis, the cell wants the **concentration** of water in the cell to equal the concentration of water outside it. Corn syrup has a lower water concentration than an egg. So the water moved out of the egg, making it shrivel up. The opposite happened with the egg in the water. The egg had a lower water concentration inside than there was outside. Water moved into the egg, making it bigger.

dissolve—to disappear into something
concentration—strength of a solution

Beady DNA

Get crafty, and make some science you can use. With this twisted key chain, you'll never forget what you're made of.

Supplies

- ruler
- scissors
- 2 6-inch (15 cm) pieces of leather jewelry cord
- beading thread
- 4-millimeter beads as follows: 6 black, 6 white, 3 blue, 3 yellow, 2 green, and 2 orange
- key ring

1. Measure and cut two pieces of leather cord. Tie a knot in the end of each piece of cord. Put one black bead on each cord. Then string one white bead onto each cord.

2. Measure and cut a 12-inch (30-cm) piece of beading thread. On the thread, string six beads in this order: white, black, blue, yellow, black, white. Lay the thread and beads flat on the table.

3 Put one piece of leather cord through one of the black beads on the thread. Then put the same cord through the next white bead. Repeat with the other leather cord and black and white beads.

4 Keeping the ends of the beading thread and the leather cord even, pull all the beads toward the knots on the bottoms of the cords. Your beads should look like an "H."

5 Pull the beading thread toward the center, between the two leather cords. On the right part of the thread, add an orange bead. On the left side, add a green bead.

6 Thread the right piece of thread through the green bead from top to bottom. Thread the left piece of thread through the orange bead from top to bottom.

continue on next page

7 Add a black and then a white bead to the left thread. Put the left leather cord through these beads. Repeat with the right cord.

8 Repeat steps 5–7 with the remaining beads. Alternate pairs of orange and green beads with yellow and blue beads.

9 Push all of the black and white beads toward the knots in the leather cords. Tie all pieces of leather cording and thread together at the top. Thread the key ring through the pieces of leather cord and tie them again.

10 Trim the ends of the cord and thread close to the knots.

11 The DNA molecule is shaped like a twisted ladder. To make this shape, twist the bottom of your model to the right. Tie small pieces of thread around the spots where the cords cross each other. Trim the ends of the thread.

Insider Info

Look closely at your key chain. You're holding a DNA model. DNA is a molecule that carries the instructions for building a living thing. It also keeps living things alive and functioning. Nearly every cell in your body has about 2 yards (1.8 m) of DNA. But it's so skinny and folded up that you can't see it without a powerful microscope. So biologists use models like the one you've just made to help them picture DNA.

DNA is made up of two long strands of sugars and phosphates. These chemicals provide structure for the molecule. In your model, the black beads represent the phosphates. The white beads show the sugars. The colorful beads stand for DNA's **base pairs**. The way the pairs are arranged is the **genetic code**. The order of these base pairs gives the instructions that organisms need to stay alive.

base pair—two joined chemicals that form the rungs of the DNA ladder
genetic code—the chemical arrangement of DNA that is passed down from generation to generation

Banana DNA

The structure of a DNA molecule is impossible to see with the naked eye. But if you could remove all the DNA from each of your trillions of cells, you could see a pile of it. Since you'd be very unhappy if your DNA were removed, let's take some from a banana instead.

Supplies

- 4 teaspoons (20 mL) rubbing alcohol
- banana
- quart-size zip-top plastic bag
- liquid measuring cup
- ¼ cup plus 2 tablespoons (90 mL) distilled water, divided
- measuring spoons
- 2 teaspoons (10 mL) dishwashing soap
- 2 small plastic cups
- ½ teaspoon (2.5 mL) salt
- craft stick
- coffee filter
- rubber band
- small, thin drinking glass
- bamboo skewer

1. For this process to work, the alcohol needs to be very, very cold. Put the bottle of rubbing alcohol into the freezer for one to two hours before you begin.

2. Peel the banana and put half of it into a zip-top plastic bag. Measure and add ¼ cup (60 mL) water to the bag.

3 Seal the bag and mash the banana and water mixture for three minutes. Make sure all the chunks are gone, and you're left with a smooth paste.

4 Measure and pour the dishwashing soap into one of the plastic cups. Measure and add the salt and 2 tablespoons (30 mL) water to the cup. Stir slowly with a craft stick until everything is well mixed, and the salt is dissolved. Try to avoid bubbles as much as possible.

5 Measure and add 2 teaspoons (10 mL) mashed up banana/water mixture to the soap solution. Stir slowly for five minutes. Again, try to avoid bubbles as much as possible.

6 Place a coffee filter on top of the other plastic cup. Allow the filter to dip into the cup, but don't allow it to touch the bottom. Put a rubber band around the top of the filter to keep it in place.

continue on next page

7 Pour the banana/soap mixture into the coffee filter. Wait 10 minutes to allow all the liquid to drip out of the coffee filter. Remove the filter. Put 2 teaspoons (10 mL) of the liquid into the thin drinking glass.

8 Take the alcohol from the freezer. Measure and slowly pour alcohol down the side of the jar. Don't pour too quickly. You don't want the alcohol and banana liquid to mix. The alcohol should make a layer on top of the banana/soap liquid. Let the layers stand for five minutes. A white jellylike substance should form between the layers.

9 Use the bamboo skewer to scoop up the white jellylike goo that forms. You've skewered some banana DNA.

Insider Info

All living things contain DNA within their cells. An individual DNA molecule contained within a single cell is too small to see. But a banana has billions of cells. When the DNA from a lot of those cells clumps together, you can see it and pick it up. Mashing the banana helped break up the banana cells. With the cells broken apart, the other chemicals could extract the DNA.

Cell membranes are made up of fats. The dishwashing soap broke down the fats just like it breaks down grease on dishes. With the membrane broken, the alcohol could get to the DNA inside. DNA will dissolve in water, but it won't dissolve in alcohol. When the alcohol touched the DNA, a solid was formed. The salt in the soap/water mixture helped the DNA molecules clump together. The clumping allowed you to see and pick up the DNA. That solid on the end of your skewer holds the instructions nature needs to make a banana.

Glossary

absorb (ab-ZORB)—to soak up

base pair (BAYS PAIR)—two joined chemicals that form the rungs of the DNA ladder

capacity (kuh-PASS-uh-tee)—the total amount something can hold

cell (SEL)—the smallest unit of a living thing

concentration (kahn-suhn-TRAY-shuhn)—the strength of a solution

dissolve (di-ZOLV)—to disappear into something else

enzyme (EN-zime)—a protein that helps break down food

evaporate (i-VA-puh-rayt)—to change from a liquid into a vapor or a gas

genetic code (juh-NET-ik KODE)—the chemical arrangement of DNA that is passed down from generation to generation

molecule (MOL-uh-kyool)—the atoms making up the smallest unit of a substance

mucous membrane (MYOO-kuhss MEM-brayn)—a soft tissue in the body that creates a slimy fluid called mucus that coats the inside of a person's breathing passages

protein (PROH-teen)—a chemical found in cells that carries out various functions that are necessary for life

Read More

Bardhan-Quallen, Sudipta. *Kitchen Science Experiments: How Does Your Mold Garden Grow?* Mad Science. New York: Sterling, 2010.

Calhoun, Yael. *Plant and Animal Science Fair Projects, Revised and Expanded Using the Scientific Method.* Biology Science Projects Using the Scientific Method. Berkeley Heights, N.J.: Enslow Publishers, 2010.

Cook, Trevor. *Experiments with Plants and Other Living Things.* Science Lab. New York: PowerKids Press, 2009.

Internet Sites

FactHound offers a safe, fun way to find Internet sites related to this book. All of the sites on FactHound have been researched by our staff.

Here's all you do:

Visit www.facthound.com

Type in this code: 9781429676762

Check out projects, games and lots more at www.capstonekids.com

Index

airborne particles, 12–13

breathing, 4, 9, 12

cells, 9, 21
    membranes of, 21, 29
chunking, 17

depth perception, 10–11
DNA, 25, 26, 29
    structure of, 25, 26

ecosystems, 15
enzymes, 19
evaporation, 7

lung capacity, 8–9

mucous membranes, 13

osmosis, 21

plants, 4, 6–7, 14–15
    stomata in, 7
proteins, 19

short-term memory, 16–17

terrariums, 14–15